5 QUALITIES OF A *Woman* of *Destiny*

TARSHA L. CAMPBELL

Copyright © 2004, 2007 by Tarsha L. Campbell
ISBN-13: 978-0-9755234-1-4
ISBN-10: 0-9755234-1-4
First Printing 2004
Second Printing 2007, revised
Third Printing 2008, revised
Fourth Printing 2010, revised

All Rights Reserved. No part of this book may be reproduced or transmitted in any form or by any means, electronically or mechanically, including photocopying, recording or by an information storage and retrieval system without permission in writing from the author of this book.

Unless otherwise indicated, all scripture quotations are taken from the King James Version of the Holy Bible.

Verses marked Amplified Bible are taken from the Amplified Bible, Copyright © 1954, 1958, 1962, 1964, 1965, 1987 by The Lockman Foundation. Used with permission.

Cover & Interior Design by Tarsha L. Campbell
Edited by Donna L. Ferrier
Proofread by Sharlyne Thomas & Ayana Campbell
Author's Photo by Michael Cairns

Published by:
DOMINIONHOUSE
Publishing & Design
P.O. Box 681938
Orlando, Florida 32868
407.880.5790 phone/fax
www.mydominionhouse.com
****

The Lord gave the word: great was the company of those that published it. (Psalms 68:11)

Praise for
5 Qualities of a Woman of Destiny

☙❧

5 Qualities of a Woman of Destiny is a book of love, restoration, great wisdom, impartation and understanding. I would encourage women worldwide to read the treasures within. In doing so, the Lord will seal his revelation to your heart and cause you to remember! I assure you that you will be comforted, healed and encouraged by the Lord through these pages. The dream and the vision growing on the inside of you will burn with a fresh fire, and you will be empowered to complete the course. Surely, through these pages, the Lord will reveal to you – as he did to me – just how precious, unique and valued you are to Him and His Kingdom. Truly, we are women of destiny and the Lord desires each one of us to be established in present truth.

Prophetess Theresa Harvard Johnson
Voices of Christ Literary
Ministries International, Inc.

5 Qualities of a Woman of Destiny reminds me that although I have been in ministry for over 25 years, there are still things I can learn and focus on. Tarsha Campbell relays the message of faith, submission, and obedience as though she is taking the reader by the hand. I not only recommend this book to every woman seeking to advance in God's call on her life, but to every leader who wants to make and impact as well as teach other women to excel in their destinies.

Pastor Gail Gardner
Woman to Woman Global Mentorship, Inc.

Dedication

*This book is dedicated to every
Woman of Destiny I have encountered
throughout my life. Through their example,
I have been inspired to pray fervently,
push harder and dream bigger!
For this impartation I am eternally grateful.*

*A true Woman of Destiny
is in tune with her Creator
and dances to the rhythm
of the life He has
created for her.*

—T.L. Campbell

Table of Contents

Foreword:
By Dr. Maureen Anderson 9

Introduction:
What is Destiny? 11

Quality #1:
She Fears Not......................... 23

Quality #2:
She Beholds the Gifts Within Herself and
Walks in Agreement with God's Plan 35

Quality #3:
She Stirs Up the Gifts in Other Women 47

Quality #4:
She is Blessed Because She Believes,
Submits and Obeys 57

Quality #5:
Her Life Magnifies and Brings
Praise to God 71

About the Author 81

More Resources 84

*D*estiny is no matter of chance. It is a matter of choice: It is not a thing to be waited for, it is a thing to be achieved."

—William Jennings Bryan

Foreword

We are all Women of Destiny on a journey and, author, Tarsha Campbell, in her book *5 Qualities of a Woman of Destiny*, gives us step-by-step instructions on how to walk in that destiny. Tarsha reveals that as women, as nurturers, we have the power and obligation to support each other in our search for destiny. We should edify the gifts in others, not be jealous of them - that is a trick of the enemy. In the world we are taught to look out for number one. In God's Kingdom, we are also taught to look after number one - our Lord and Savior Jesus Christ. We must look to Him to fulfill our purpose. He is the only one who can guide us on this journey. *5 Qualities of a Woman of Destiny* will put you on the path to YOUR purpose and destiny in Christ. The meditations and the confessions in this book are an excellent tools to succeed in this journey to destiny. Be blessed!

Dr. Maureen Anderson
Founder of *Women of Destiny Ministries*
Living Word Bible Church, Mesa, Arizona

Watch your thoughts,

for they become words.

Watch your words,

for they become actions.

Watch your actions,

for they become habits.

Watch your habits,

for they become character.

Watch your character, for it

becomes your destiny.

—Anonymous

Introduction
ಸಬಲ

What is Destiny?

In recent years, we've heard so much talk about destiny. Statements such as, *"God has called you to destiny," "Walk in your destiny," "Move toward your destiny,"* and *"You have a destiny,"* have flooded our world. In the midst of all this talk, I've often thought to myself, *"Yeah, I hear what you're saying, but can someone please explain to me exactly what destiny is and how it affects my life?"* Have you ever felt like this, too? Or am I all alone in my thinking? As I began to search for answers, my quest started with a guy named Webster.

Tucked away within the pages of Webster's Dictionary, I found the definition of *destiny* sandwiched between *destine* and *destitute*. The first definition reads:

5 Qualities of a Woman of Destiny

> (1) The inevitable loss or fate to which a person or thing is destined.

"Okay," I said to myself, as I tried to wrap my brain around what I had just read. I knew immediately that if I was going to make sense of this first definition I needed to break the words down into phrases I could comprehend. After all, what in the world did *inevitable* mean? And what exactly is *fate?* I had heard the words before, but they just weren't clicking with me.

So I looked up both *inevitable* and *fate,* and I must report the word *destiny* was still a mystery. So I read the second definition of destiny provided by my friend, Mr. Webster:

> (2) A predetermined course of events.

Introduction: What is Destiny?

All right! Now, I was starting to feel something! As I read the definition over and over, it seemed to roll over and over in my spirit and stir my inner being. It reminded me of jumpstarting a car. First, you connect the cable to the live battery. Then, just before you connect the cable to the dead battery of the other car, you bring the two clamps together, causing sparks to fly. This second definition was definitely causing some sparks to fly. I knew I was on to something profound. Then my eyes fell on the word *destination*, two words up from the word *destiny*:

> The point or place to which something or someone is directed; the purpose to which something is created or designed.

By this time my spirit was revved up as if it was about to speed down a spiritual race track.

As I looked at the dictionary again, my eyes fell upon another word sandwiched right between *destination* and *destiny*. The word was *destine*. Destine is a verb (an action word). When I examined it more closely, I discovered that it seems to be the root word to both *destination* and *destiny*. The definition moved me again inwardly:

> To be determined in advance; to design or appoint for a distinct purpose.

I knew at this moment that the Holy Spirit wanted to speak. Without a doubt, I felt that destiny was a part of God's plan for my life. I also felt I had to know what destiny was, and specifically, what it meant for my life. My natural mind thought it had grasped the meaning of destiny to some degree through Mr. Webster's definitions, but my spiritual mind reached to the Spirit for more. I then asked the

Introduction: What is Destiny?

golden question, *"Holy Spirit, what is destiny?"*

The Spirit spoke. (Side note: You do know the Spirit still speaks if we ask and quiet our thinking mind to hear Him, don't you? Matthew 7:7-8 says, "Ask, and it shall be given you; seek, and you shall find; knock, and the door shall be opened to you…") This is what I heard the Spirit say. Are you ready?

Destiny is a God-appointed person, going to a God-appointed place, at a God-appointed time, for a God-appointed purpose.

My natural mind said, "What?", but my spiritual mind bore witness with the Spirit and said, "Yes!" At this point, I felt completely connected and energized by this newfound definition delivered straight from the throne room of heaven!

5 Qualities of a Woman of Destiny

I now understand destiny in a whole new light. I am a Woman of Destiny! You are a Woman of Destiny! We have been appointed by God. We were fashioned, made and created for a specific purpose. Just as the Word of God came to Jeremiah in Jeremiah 1:5, we must grab hold of this truth for ourselves. I love how this scripture reads from the Amplified Bible:

> Before I formed you in the womb I knew [and] approved of you [as My chosen instrument], and before you were born I separated and set you apart, consecrating you; [and] I appointed you as a prophet to the nations.

As a Woman of Destiny, you must realize it doesn't matter which lie the devil has told you about your conception: "You weren't planned," "The birth control failed," "You were an accident," "Your life doesn't count for anything"

Introduction: What is Destiny?

or "You're a product of some unfortunate event." The list goes on. You must realize the truth: you are a God-appointed person, going to a God-appointed place, at a God-appointed time, for a God-appointed purpose. God knew you and predestined you for His purpose. God had you on His mind even before your mother knew you or before your father was moved by his raging hormones. *You were predestined for God's purpose!* Look at Romans 8:28-30 in the Amplified Bible. I love this passage of scripture:

> We are assured and know that [God being a partner in their labor] all things work together and are [fitting into a plan] for good to and for those who love God and are called according to [His] design and purpose. For those whom He foreknew [of whom He was aware and loved beforehand],

He also destined from the beginning [foreordaining them] to be molded into the image of His Son [and share inwardly His likeness], that He might become the firstborn among many brethren. And those whom He thus foreordained, He also called; and those whom He called, He also justified (acquitted, made righteous, putting them into right standing with Himself). And those whom He justified, He also glorified [raising them to a heavenly dignity and condition or state of being].

My sister, you have been appointed by God for a specific purpose. Destiny is calling! Can you hear it calling your name? As a Woman of Destiny, you must fine tune your spiritual ears and declare the Word of the Lord according to Psalms 139:13-18:

> For thou hast possessed my reins: thou hast covered me in my mother's womb.

Introduction: What is Destiny?

I will praise thee; for I am fearfully and wonderfully made: marvellous are thy works; and that my soul knoweth right well. My substance was not hid from thee, when I was made in secret, and curiously wrought in the lowest parts of the earth. Thine eyes did see my substance, yet being unperfect; and in thy book all my members were written, which in continuance were fashioned, when as yet there was none of them. How precious also are thy thoughts unto me, O God! how great is the sum of them! If I should count them, they are more in number than the sand: when I awake, I am still with thee.

Now that we know what destiny is, together let's explore the 5 Qualities of a Woman of Destiny. We will examine the life of an extraordinary God-appointed woman who embraced her destiny and changed the course of history for all mankind.

Introduction: What is Destiny?

Prayer For Impartation

Father, I now pray as we enter this study that you allow your Spirit to speak profoundly to my sister. Lord, release an anointing that makes it easy to read and understand the truth found within these pages. Holy Spirit, have your free course and cause the eyes of the reader to be enlightened, stirring up every gift, talent, dream and destiny within them. Allow the Word to fall on good ground and bring forth much fruit for the glory and praise of the eternal kingdom of God. For this divine impartation we will be so grateful. So be the Word of the Lord this day! In Jesus' name, Amen.

The key to change...

is to let go of fear.

—Rosanne Cash

QUALITY 1

She Fears Not

Woman of Destiny, arise! Your time has come! The Word of the Lord has been spoken! *Your day is at hand, but do you have what it takes?*

As a Woman of Destiny, you must possess certain qualities. Throughout the Bible, God has given us examples of women who were called and chosen for a specific purpose. One such woman was Mary, the mother of our Savior.

Mary was truly a Woman of Destiny. As I began to study her story in Luke 1, beginning in verse 26, God began speaking to me about the 5 Qualities of a Woman of Destiny. The first quality is found in Luke 1:30: "And the angel said unto her, *Fear not,* Mary: for thou hast found favor with God." In this verse, the angel says to Mary, "Fear not." The first quality of a Woman of Destiny is: She fears not.

All of us at some point in our lives have experienced fear. As I closely examined the concept of fear, I came to realize there are several types, some of which are beneficial, and others that are detrimental.

The first type of fear is reverential fear, which speaks of reverence and respect, and is described in Proverbs 1:7, "The fear of the Lord is the beginning of knowledge: but fools despise wisdom and instruction." Reverential fear is beneficial because it humbles the soul and gets God's attention.

The second type of fear is the kind of anxiety we may experience when we're in danger, such as when we pass a vicious dog on the street.

Quality #1: She Fears Not

This kind of fear, in most cases, is beneficial because it allows us to prepare a defense to ensure our safety or the safety of others.

The final type of fear is the kind that causes dread. This is the kind of fear that the enemy uses to keep us from reaching our destiny because it leaves us paralyzed, powerless and ineffective.

Mark 4:35-41 gives us a vivid picture of this kind of fear in action. The passage gives an account of Jesus with His disciples as they set out to reach a specific destination. Jesus said to them, "Let us pass over unto the other side." Then Jesus and His disciples set sail, and a great storm arose, tossing the boat to and fro. Jesus was below deck sleeping while all this was going on. In a state of panic, the disciples woke Him and asked whether He cared if they perished. Jesus simply arose, rebuked the wind and said to the sea, "Peace, be still," and it obeyed. Jesus then turned to the disciples and rebuked them: *"Why are ye so fearful? How is it that ye have no faith?"*

Now let's analyze this scenario for one moment. In all likelihood, the disciples were used to sea voyages, and rough seas were probably common to them. In this case, however, they allowed their circumstances to become their focus. Fear overtook them, which hindered their ability to function and progress.

The Woman of Destiny can similarly succumb to fear when she takes her focus off of her destination and purpose. When we allow fear to overtake us, we quickly lose faith and doubt the power of God within us to reach a goal or destination. The enemy loves to use fear to trick us into diverting our attention away from our God-given destiny (destination) and purpose. Satan frequently uses the fear of man (the sea

Quality #1: She Fears Not

sometimes symbolically represents man) to cause us to abort our mission. At those times, we must remember who we have on board and exercise the power within us to calm our fears. To paraphrase 1 John 4:4, greater is He within you than he that is in the world.

God knew that fear would be a big obstacle to us when we pursue our destiny. Throughout scripture, whenever God called someone to a specific purpose, He would say to them, "Fear not," or "Don't be afraid." One biblical scholar noted that the scriptures contain 80 occurrences of "Fear not."

God told Abraham in Genesis 26:24 to "Fear not," as He revealed his destiny. Similarly, He told Joshua in Joshua 1:9 to "Be strong and of good courage; be not afraid," as he entered into his destiny as Israel's new leader. And when we look at the New Testament, we discover that God told someone else besides Mary to "Fear not." Luke 1:13 reads, "But the angel said unto him, Fear not, Zacharias: for thy prayer is heard; and thy wife Elisabeth shall bear thee a son, and thou shalt call his name John."

Unfortunately, even though the angel told Zacharias to "Fear not," Zacharias still allowed fear to fill his mind, as the messenger revealed God's destiny for him in verses 18-25. Consequently, Zacharias' fear caused him to doubt that God could actually fulfill His promise to him and his wife, Elisabeth.

Fear and doubt work hand in hand, and the enemy knows this. Satan tries to get us to fear because he knows it will open the door to doubt—a major hindrance to fulfilling our destiny. 2 Corinthians 10:4-5 states:

> For the weapons of our warfare are not carnal, but mighty through God to the pulling down

Quality #1: She Fears Not

of strong holds; Casting down imaginations, and every high thing that exalteth itself against the knowledge of God, and bringing into captivity every thought to the obedience of Christ.

Fear and doubt are evil imaginations that keep us from our destiny. Even though there are times in my life when fear tries to grip my mind, I simply remind myself of the absolute faithfulness of God's Word and stand upon it. Standing upon God's Word is one of the weapons we have as Women of Destiny because the Word is ammunition to combat fear and doubt. 2 Timothy 1:7 says, "For God hath not given us the spirit of fear; but of power, and of love, and of a sound mind."

The Woman of Destiny must constantly remind herself that God's power and love brings peace (a sound mind). Isaiah 26:3 tells us that God will keep us in perfect peace, when our minds are stayed on Him, because we trust in Him. The peace to fulfill our destiny is released when we guard our minds against fear and doubt. When the Woman of Destiny focuses on the Word of God and permits faith to rise, she then becomes an unstoppable force against the enemy!

Dear sister, as Women of Destiny, we must purpose in our hearts that we will not allow fear and doubt to rule us. Mary wasn't moved by her circumstances or the opinion of man. She clearly refused to fear and doubt the Word the Lord gave her. Mary was strong in faith and believed her God. She knew He would fulfill His destiny for her life and did not fear. Now this is truly a quality of a Woman of Destiny!

Quality #1: She Fears Not

Personal Reflections

Dear sister, take some time and reflect upon the questions below, responding quietly within yourself or within a journal.

1) What is the first quality of a Woman of Destiny?

2) Are there areas in your life where you are fearful?

3) If so, how has the fear affected your life?

4) What do you stand to gain by walking in fear?

5) What do you stand to gain by walking in faith?

6) Find and memorize two scriptures to help you combat fear in your life.

Meditation For Activation

Meditate upon the following scriptures to gain and maintain greater success in your life.

Psalms 37:3 — Trust in the LORD, and do good; so shalt thou dwell in the land, and verily thou shalt be fed.

Proverbs 14:26 — In the fear of the LORD is strong confidence: and his children shall have a place of refuge.

Philippians 1:6 — Being confident of this very thing, that he which hath begun a good work in you will perform it until the day of Jesus Christ.

Hebrews 10:35 — Cast not away therefore your confidence, which hath great recompence of reward.

Quality #1: She Fears Not

Confession For Possession

I declare and decree, according to I Timothy 1:7, that God has not given me the spirit of fear, but a spirit of power, and of love and of a sound mind. I denounce every power of the enemy that seeks to use fear and intimidation to rob me of my God-given destiny. I stand in agreement with the Word of God that I'm empowered to possess every promise the Father has for me. I know without a doubt according to 1 John 4:4 that greater is He that is within me than he that is in the world, therefore I refuse to walk and live in fear! So be the Word of the Lord this day! In Jesus' name, Amen.

*Believe in your dreams
and they may come true;
believe in yourself
and they will come true.*

— *Anonymous*

QUALITY

She Beholds the Gifts Within Herself and Walks in Agreement with God's Plan

Now on to the second quality of a Woman of Destiny. Let's go back to our scripture in Luke 1, beginning in verses 31-38:

> And, behold, thou shalt conceive in thy womb, and bring forth a son, and shalt call his name Jesus. He shall be great, and shall be called the Son of the Highest: and the Lord God shall give unto him the throne of his father David: And he shall reign over the house of Jacob for ever; and of his kingdom there shall be no end. Then said Mary unto the angel, How shall this be, seeing I know not a

man? And the angel answered and said unto her, The Holy Ghost shall come upon thee, and the power of the Highest shall overshadow thee: therefore also that holy thing which shall be born of thee shall be called the Son of God. And, behold, thy cousin Elisabeth, she hath also conceived a son in her old age: and this is the sixth month with her, who was called barren. For with God nothing shall be impossible. And Mary said, Behold the handmaid of the Lord; be it unto me according to thy word. And the angel departed from her.

Within these verses we will find the second quality of a Woman of Destiny: She beholds the gifts within herself and walks in agreement with God's plan.

In these verses, the angel of the Lord reveals to Mary God's wonderful purpose for her existence.

Quality #2: She Beholds the Gifts Within Herself and Walks in Agreement with God's Plan

As the Word came to her, she probably looked around the room and said, *"Are you talking to me?"* This is so typical of all of us. God has a way of shocking our world when He reveals such a grandiose plan for our life.

Have you ever noticed when He reveals His plan, there is absolutely no sign, or even an inkling, that it can be accomplished using your own strength? Most of the time when He speaks to you concerning your destiny, your current situation doesn't give any clue that it can be done! The same was true for Mary.

In verse 31, God had the audacity to tell Mary (a virgin, I might add), "Hey, I have a plan for your life. You're going to conceive in your womb and have a baby. Oh, one more thing— He's my son whom I promised to send to save the world." Can you imagine what Mary must have thought and felt? There she was, minding her own business, going about her day and—BAM!—she receives a tremendous Word from the Lord that would transform her life forever!

In verse 34, Mary began to question God: "How shall this be, seeing I know not a man?" From this verse, we can see how Mary began to evaluate her situation, as she says, *"Okay I hear you, but have you forgotten that I do have some limitations?"*

So often, we respond just like Mary did when God declares His destiny to us: *"How can this be?" "I haven't been to college," "I don't have the money," "I'm not the right color," "I'm too fat," "I'm too skinny"* or *"I have too many kids."* And the list goes on.

Too often the enemy uses your own mind to derail the plan of God for your life. But you

*Quality #2: She Beholds the Gifts Within Herself
and Walks in Agreement with God's Plan*

must understand that the mind is a battlefield, and as a Woman of Destiny, you must be aware of the tactics of the enemy. And the enemy isn't always the devil. Sometimes the negative thoughts you have about yourself hinder you from reaching your full potential. Paraphrasing Proverbs 23:7, *for as a man thinketh in his heart, so is he.*

You must come to realize the power of your thoughts and use them to your advantage. To fully understand this, you need to see your mind as a womb. When I speak of the mind, I'm not talking about your physical brain that helps you process natural things. Rather, I'm speaking of the inward spirit of man.

This is the place where the Word of the Lord concerning your life should be conceived. Most of the time when the Word comes, however, we like to process it with our natural minds, rather than letting it take root in our spirit.

What you must understand, however, is that man has two minds at work, according to Romans 8:5-8, the fleshly (or natural) mind and the spiritual mind. When the Word is planted in your spirit, conception takes place. Upon conception, we must allow our thoughts to be coupled with faith to birth the manifestation of this Word.

In Luke 1:34-38, Mary switches gears from, "How shall this be, seeing..." (fleshly mind), to "Behold the handmaid of the Lord; be it unto me according to thy word" (spiritual mind). When she bridged this transition, Mary clearly exhibited the second quality of a Woman of Destiny. She didn't settle for walking according to the flesh or according to her natural circumstances. Verse 35 indicates that she was willing to step into the supernatural by allowing the Word of the Lord to be deposited inside her womb or spirit.

*Quality #2: She Beholds the Gifts Within Herself
and Walks in Agreement with God's Plan*

In addition, Mary not only aligned her spirit and her thoughts, but she also aligned her mouth, too! Verse 38 begins, "And Mary said…." As a Woman of Destiny, you must be careful to speak only those things that the Father has spoken. Proverbs 18:21 says, *"Death and life are in the power of the tongue: and they that love it shall eat the fruit thereof."*

Mary was able to place value on the seed, or the Word, that came to her. She didn't discard or abort the Word because of unbelief or negative speaking. Instead, Mary was taken to another level — or dare I say, "realm" — because of her faith. When true revelation came to her and she realized in verse 37, "With God nothing shall be impossible," her faith soared. This point must be embraced in your walk as a Woman of Destiny: *true revelation brings elevation.*

Dear sister, please hear me! As a Woman of Destiny, you must behold or perceive the gift of

God within you. Colossians 1:27 says that it's "Christ in you, the hope of glory." And 2 Corinthians 4:7 reads, "But we have this treasure in earthen vessels, that the excellency of the power may be of God, and not of us."

My sister, open your eyes and behold the gift(s) within you. For when you are able to see the tremendous gift of God implanted within you through the Spirit's eyes, and walk in agreement with it, you will give birth to your awesome purpose just like Mary. This is definitely a quality of a Woman of Destiny that must be embraced, cultivated and practiced!

*Quality #2: She Beholds the Gifts Within Herself
and Walks in Agreement with God's Plan*

Personal Reflections

Dear sister, take some time and reflect upon the questions below, responding quietly within yourself or within a journal.

1) What is the second quality of a Woman of Destiny?

2) Make a list of the gifts God has placed in your life. What are you doing to develop them?

3) How has the enemy used your own mind to derail the plan of God for your life?

4) What do you think would have happened if Mary didn't behold the gift within her and walk in agreement with it?

5) What do you think will happen to you if you fail to behold the gift within you and walk in agreement with it?

5 Qualities of a Woman of Destiny

Meditation For Activation

Meditate upon the following scriptures to gain and maintain greater success in your life.

Proverbs 17:8 — A gift is as a precious stone in the eyes of him that hath it: whithersoever it turneth, it prospereth.

Proverbs 18:16 — A man's gift maketh room for him, and bringeth him before great men.

James 1:17 — Every good gift and every perfect gift is from above, and cometh down from the Father of lights, with whom is no variableness, neither shadow of turning.

1 Peter 4:10 — As every man hath received the gift, even so minister the same one to another, as good stewards of the manifold grace of God.

*Quality #2: She Beholds the Gifts Within Herself
and Walks in Agreement with God's Plan*

Confession For Possession

I declare and decree I will behold the gifts within me. I refuse to allow them to lay dormant in my life. My gifts have been deposited into my life for a specific God-given purpose. I will, therefore, make every effort to develop them so the Father may be glorified. I deny the enemy of my destiny any right to keep me from cultivating my gifts and talents. I also guard my mind and mouth against any negative self-thinking and talking, for I know this hinders my progress. I stand in agreement with 2 Peter 1:3-11 and believe according to the divine power that works in me. I move forward and grow more mature each time I use my gifts for God's purpose and glory. So be the Word of the Lord this day! In Jesus' name, Amen.

The most important thing women have to do is to stir up the zeal of women themselves.

—John Stuart Mill

QUALITY

She Stirs Up the Gifts In Other Women

I know by now you're starting to get a clearer picture of what it takes to be a Woman of Destiny. To bring the picture into clearer focus, let's go back to our reference scripture, Luke 1, and look at verses 39-41:

> And Mary arose in those days, and went into the hill country with haste, into a city of Judah; And entered into the house of Zacharias, and saluted Elisabeth. And it came to pass, that, when Elisabeth heard the salutation of Mary, the babe leaped in her womb; and Elisabeth was filled with the Holy Ghost.

Within this passage of scripture, we find the third quality of a Woman of Destiny: She stirs up the gifts in other women. Here, we definitely see how exceptional Mary really was. A closer examination reveals what sets her apart from others.

Mary was excited because she had just received a Word from the Lord about her destiny. She was so excited that she wanted to share it with others, so she decided to visit her cousin, Elisabeth. Now think for a moment. Mary had just received her Word, and there were no physical signs that she was impregnated with destiny. On the other hand, Elisabeth received the Word about her destiny and the gift she carried six months prior to Mary's visit.

Luke 1:8-25 indicates that the angel came to Elisabeth's house before coming to Mary's and told Elisabeth that she would give birth

Quality #3: She Stirs Up the Gifts In Other Women

to John the Baptist (the forerunner of Jesus). So there's no doubt that Elisabeth already manifested physical signs of her destiny by the time Mary arrived. Luke 1:40 says that when Mary entered Elisabeth's house, she saluted her. Now salute is an old English word for greet. In other words, Mary greeted or acknowledged Elisabeth when she entered. In my spirit, as I read between the lines, I feel this wasn't a common greeting. I get the feeling that when Mary saw Elisabeth's condition and the physical signs of her destiny manifested, she was able to acknowledge and connect with her in the Spirit and rejoice!

So often I see in the body of Christ, at least among women, the disregard we have for each other's destinies. Most of the time this negative reaction is birthed from a spirit of jealousy, intimidation or a combination of both. When we allow these spirits to dominate us, we tend to fight against what God is doing through our sister(s), rather than build them up. This is another trick of the enemy to stop us from fulfilling our destinies.

The devil knows that if he can control you, using jealousy and intimidation, and get you to fight against your sisters, he will stand a greater chance of aborting the plan of God in your life. This is why you must practice stirring up the gift(s) in other women.

Mary wasn't moved by jealousy, nor was she intimidated by the gift in Elisabeth. Instead, she was excited about the way God was working in Elisabeth, which Mary clearly exhibited upon entering her home. The point here is that even though Mary wasn't yet fully walking in her destiny, she was still able to greet Elisabeth with excitement. Through this excitement, Mary caused a stirring, which

Quality #3: She Stirs Up the Gifts In Other Women

catapulted Elisabeth to a new level in the Spirit. Luke 1:41 states that Elisabeth was filled with the Holy Ghost right there on the spot!

> And it came to pass, that, when Elisabeth heard the salutation of Mary, the babe leaped in her womb; and Elisabeth was filled with the Holy Ghost.

In fact, verses 42-45 indicate that Mary stirred up the gift so much that Elisabeth began to prophesy:

> And she spake out with a loud voice, and said, Blessed art thou among women, and blessed is the fruit of thy womb. And whence is this to me, that the mother of my Lord should come to me? For, lo, as soon as the voice of thy salutation sounded in mine ears, the babe leaped in my womb for joy. And blessed is she that believed: for there shall be

a performance of those things which were told her from the Lord.

After Mary stirred up the gift in Elisabeth, God then used Elisabeth to bless Mary. This is why we can't be so self-absorbed and preoccupied with our own emotions, interests and situations that we neglect to help others embrace their destinies. I have personally found my destiny contained in the unveiling of another person's destiny. I once heard a preacher say, *"Whatever you make happen for someone else, God will make happen for you."* A true Woman of Destiny knows this; that's why she isn't afraid to help build the dreams of others. For in doing so, she knows God will unfold her destiny in due season. Galatians 6:7 declares, "Be not deceived; God is not mocked: for whatsoever a man soweth, that shall he also reap."

Quality #3: She Stirs Up the Gifts In Other Women

Personal Reflections

Dear sister, take some time and reflect upon the questions below, responding quietly within yourself or within a journal.

1) What is the third quality of a Woman of Destiny?

2) Do you find yourself jealous or intimidated by other women and the gifts God has placed in their lives? If so, what has been your response to them?

3) What do we accomplish as women when we fight and war against each other? How do we overcome spirits of jealousy and intimidation?

4) What happens when we acknowledge, exhort, encourage and stir up the gifts in our sisters in our families, workplaces, churches and ministries?

Meditation For Activation

Meditate upon the following scriptures to gain and maintain greater success in your life.

Proverbs 27:17 — Iron sharpeneth iron; so a man sharpeneth the countenance of his friend.

Song of Solomon 8:8-10 — We have a little sister, and she hath no breasts: what shall we do for our sister in the day when she shall be spoken for? If she be a wall, we will build upon her a palace of silver: and if she be a door, we will inclose her with boards of cedar. I am a wall, and my breasts like towers: then was I in his eyes as one that found favour.

2 Peter 1:13 — Yea, I think it meet, as long as I am in this tabernacle, to stir you up by putting you in remembrance.

Quality #3: She Stirs Up the Gifts In Other Women

Confession For Possession

I declare and decree that I will stand confident in who I am in Christ. I will not be controlled by spirits of jealousy and intimidation, fighting against my sisters in my family, workplace, church and ministry. Since I am confident in the Father's love and believe He has created a purpose for my life, I don't have to covet any gifts or destinies appointed to my sisters. Through this confidence, I will daily acknowledge, exhort, encourage and stir up the gifts in my sisters wherever I encounter them. In doing so, God will make clear paths for me and my destiny, and nothing shall be withheld from me. I stand in agreement with Galatians 6:7, that whatsoever I sow, that shall I also reap, and I claim it done all for the glory of God. So be the Word of the Lord this day! In Jesus' name, Amen.

Everything we have today is a result of what we have thought, spoken, believed and submitted in obedience to.

—T.L. Campbell

QUALITY 4

She Is Blessed Because She Believes, Submits and Obeys

Let's move on to the fourth quality of a Woman of Destiny, which is spoken of Mary in Luke 1:45: "And blessed is she that believed: for there shall be a performance of those things which were told her from the Lord."

As a Woman of Destiny, Mary dared to believe the impossible. She was strong in faith and able to reach beyond her present situation to a greater depth in God. Even though Mary's faith allowed her to enter into another dimension, this new dimension actually required more from her in the end than her faith. A closer evaluation of her actions reveals the fourth quality of a Woman of

5 Qualities of a Woman of Destiny

Destiny: She is blessed because she believes, submits and obeys.

When the angel first appeared to Mary, he clearly made her status known in the kingdom of God. According to Luke 1:28, Mary was considered highly favoured (sometimes spelled favored). The Amplified Bible reads, "O favored one (endued with grace)." Mary was one special lady, but do you know why? It's the same reason all of us are special—because of the grace of God extended to us. Even though we know how special Mary was when we examine how she exhibited the first three qualities of a Woman of Destiny already discussed, we must not overlook the fact that Mary was a sinner, born into a world of sin. David explains in Psalms 51:5, "Behold, I was shapen in iniquity; and in sin did my mother conceive me." In other words, Mary had flaws and faults just like all of us.

*Quality #4: She Is Blessed Because She
Believes, Submits and Obeys*

Romans 3:23 says, "For all have sinned, and come short of the glory of God."

But here's where God comes in. When we fall short, God extends His favor to us and tells us that He has a destiny for us. God had a plan for Mary's life, and He knew that she had to realize her position in Him in order for her to fulfill it. This is why He instructed the angel to declare that plan in Luke 1:30 before he said anything else.

My sister, you have to embrace this! It's absolutely necessary that you realize your position in Christ when pursuing your destiny. For so long the devil has beaten many of us over the head with our past. *He uses our flaws and faults against us to detour us off the path of purpose.*

He persuades many of us to talk ourselves out of our destiny because we feel we don't qualify because of a sinful past or present. But I have a news flash for you: This is why Christ came! His death paid all your sin debts, and all you have now is God's favor (or grace) credited to your account. Merely coming to God makes this grace available to you. Hebrews 4:16 says, "Let us therefore come boldly unto the throne of grace, that we may obtain mercy, and find grace to help in time of need."

You must learn to beat Satan at his own game. 2 Corinthians 2:11 says that we are not to be ignorant of Satan's devices, lest he get the advantage over us. You have to put into practice the principles God has established in His Word for your success.

To make this point clear we can look at the life of Paul (also called Saul). He had an awful past. According to Acts 8:1, 3, he did all manner of evil against God and the church. But in spite

*Quality #4: She Is Blessed Because She
Believes, Submits and Obeys*

of all his evil doing, God still called Paul to his destiny in Acts 9:3-22! As I studied Paul's life a little closer, I discovered in Philippians 3:13-14 why he was so successful in fulfilling his destiny:

> Brethren, I count not myself to have apprehended: but this one thing I do, forgetting those things which are behind, and reaching forth unto those things which are before, I press toward the mark for the prize of the high calling of God in Christ Jesus.

Paul didn't let his past determine his future. He made a conscious decision to walk in the favor (grace) of God extended to him. As a Woman of Destiny, you must do the same.

Now back to Mary. I am sure by now you understand why Mary was highly favored. Upon closer study, however, the Spirit revealed to me that Mary was not only favored, but she was also blessed. Well, if you're like me, right now you're probably asking, *"Isn't being highly favored and blessed the same thing?"* In some cases they are similar, but the Spirit unveiled a fresh, profound revelation to me—you have to get this! The "Highly Favored Mary" was God's doing, but the "Blessed Mary" was her doing. Did you get that?

Here's how the Spirit explained it. In Luke 1:30 the angel declared to Mary her position in God, (Highly Favored Mary). As explained previously, God had extended His divine favor and grace to her. It was all His doing. But in Luke 1:45, Mary established a new position in God, which was "Blessed Mary," and she did this by believing. And because she believed, Mary was able to establish a higher position and quality of life.

But in order for Mary to rightfully claim the title "Blessed" in verse 45, she had to submit

*Quality #4: She Is Blessed Because She
Believes, Submits and Obeys*

to God's plan. In verse 38 she says, "...be it unto me according to thy Word."

Her submission to God's Word not only brought blessings to her life, but also to generations after her. As a Woman of Destiny, you must develop the ability to submit. Submission is a forerunner of obedience, and obedience brings blessings into your life. Isaiah 1:19-20 says, "If ye be willing and obedient, ye shall eat the good of the land: But if ye refuse and rebel, ye shall be devoured with the sword: for the mouth of the Lord hath spoken it."

Did you notice the consequences in verse 20 when you don't submit and obey? You would be devoured with the sword, which is a symbol of the Word of God. So the same Word of God that reveals the blessings for your life brings the exact opposite when it's handled by an unyielding and disobedient spirit. Just think for a moment. Would redemption and blessings through Christ have been made available to Mary *(or us for that matter)* if she had refused and rebelled against God's Word concerning her? I don't think so! We must realize that God isn't just trying to complete His agenda—He has our best interests at heart. The same Word (Christ) implanted in Mary's womb for God's purpose also saved her and gave her (and us) a better quality of life.

God doesn't present a half-hearted plan concerning your destiny. God is a God of love and has a master plan for you, which will bring you prosperity on all levels of your life when you submit to it. Jeremiah 29:11 says: "For I know the thoughts that I think toward you, saith the Lord, thoughts of peace, and not of evil, to give you an expected end." In the Amplified Bible, this verse reads, "For I know the thoughts and plans that I have for you, says the Lord, thoughts and plans for

*Quality #4: She Is Blessed Because She
Believes, Submits and Obeys*

welfare and peace and not for evil, to give you hope in your final outcome."

This is why a true Woman of Destiny must cultivate a spirit that's willing to believe, submit and obey. Mary had such a spirit, and this is why she was blessed. What position have you established for yourself? *Can you be called "Blessed"? Think about it.*

5 Qualities of a Woman of Destiny

Personal Reflections

Dear sister, take some time and reflect upon the questions below, responding quietly within yourself or within a journal.

1) What is the fourth quality of a Woman of Destiny?

2) What qualified Mary to be called "Highly Favoured Mary"?

3) What qualified Mary to be called "Blessed Mary"?

4) Do you feel your past or present disqualifies you from being a Woman of Destiny?

5) What helped Paul to embrace his God-given destiny? Can what he practiced help you reach your destiny?

*Quality #4: She Is Blessed Because She
Believes, Submits and Obeys*

6) How important is it to believe God's Word when fulfilling your God-given destiny?

7) How important is submission and obedience when fulfilling your God-given destiny?

8) Can God call you "Blessed"?

5 Qualities of a Woman of Destiny

Meditation For Activation

Meditate upon the following scriptures to gain and maintain greater success in your life.

Mark 9:23 — Jesus said unto him, If thou canst believe, all things are possible to him that believeth.

Romans 5:19 — For as by one man's disobedience many were made sinners, so by the obedience of one shall many be made righteous.

1 Peter 5:5-6 — Likewise, ye younger, submit yourselves unto the elder. Yea, all of you be subject one to another, and be clothed with humility: for God resisteth the proud, and giveth grace to the humble. Humble yourselves therefore under the mighty hand of God, that he may exalt you in due time.

*Quality #4: She Is Blessed Because She
Believes, Submits and Obeys*

Confession For Possession

I declare and decree that I live according to Isaiah 1:19-20. Because I am willing and obedient to God's Word for my life, I eat the good of the land. I refuse to walk in disbelief and rebel against the voice of God. I completely submit to God's will for my life, bringing my spirit, soul and body under subjection to His purpose for me. In accordance with 1 Corinthians 7:23-24, I realize that Christ bought me with a price through His precious blood, and I refuse to be a servant to the will of man (including myself) so that I may abide in the call and destiny for my life. I am called "Blessed" all the days of my life because I believe, submit and obey God's will for me. So be the Word of the Lord today! In Jesus' name, Amen.

The greatest way to magnify and praise God is to magnify and praise yourself less. As you decrease, He increases, and His glory is revealed through you, lighting the way for mankind.

—T. L. Campbell

QUALITY 5

Her Life Magnifies and Brings Praise to God

We can definitely see, at this point, what it takes to be a Woman of Destiny. Mary's life has really opened my eyes to the characteristics that a woman called to purpose must cultivate. Through this study I've come to understand that God knows exactly what He is doing when He calls us to a specific purpose and destiny. He knows what it takes to reach our God-given destinations. It was He who placed them in us from the foundation of the world. Remember the scripture from Jeremiah 1:4-5 we read at the beginning of this discourse?

> Then the word of the Lord came unto me saying, Before I formed thee in the belly I knew thee; and before thou camest forth

out of the womb I sanctified thee, and I ordained thee a prophet unto the nations.

God knew Mary had what it took; that's why He called her. God knows you have what it takes; that's why He has called you (for He was the one who placed that call in you). Now the only person who needs to confirm His Word in your life is YOU!

So often we look to people around us to confirm and validate God's Word about our destiny. But this isn't the will of God. Even though God will send prophets, pastors and mentors to confirm His Word to you, validation can only come from Him.

He is the only one who has the power to establish. This is why we don't have to worry about being a part of some social club or clique to reach our destiny. According to

*Quality #5: Her Life Magnifies and Brings
Praise to God*

Psalms 119:133, all we need to do is order our steps according to God's Word, and not the words of those around us.

Mary had a firm grip on this. This is why she was able to portray the fifth quality of a Woman of Destiny: Her life magnifies and brings praise to God.

Mary understood that God and God alone would establish her and cause her to make her mark for generations to come. Mary didn't call a board meeting to take a vote to see whether God would do what He said He would, nor did she gather her closest friends to poll their thoughts. Mary didn't even call Joseph (her fiancé) to see if he would approve it. Instead, Mary reached deep within herself and said in Luke 1:46, "My soul doth magnify the Lord." Mary knew she had a great destiny before her, and she knew where her help would come from. In fact, the source of this help can be found in Psalms 121 (study and meditate upon this passage of scripture).

Mary also knew if she was going to pull this thing off that she would need to align her soul, comprised of her mind, will and emotions, with the plan of God. This is why she said, "My soul doth magnify the Lord." If you look up the word *magnify*, you will find it means to increase the apparent size of an object. The Greek interpretation of this word means to enlarge, or to make (or declare) great.

Mary realized in order for her to walk as a Woman of Destiny, she would have to decrease her need to be validated by those around her. So, she chose to enlarge her perception of God within her. Mary began to declare in her mind, will and emotions the awesomeness of God embodied in her. She didn't magnify the

*Quality #5: Her Life Magnifies and Brings
Praise to God*

opinions of her family, her friends or her soon-to-be husband, Joseph. All she could do was magnify her God because she knew her life was in His hands!

In verse 47, Mary even went a step further as she began to declare that her spirit rejoiced in God. From this declaration we can see in Mary a woman who's totally sold out to God and His purpose. Mary aligned her whole being with God's will and was willing to lay her life before God as a living sacrifice. In doing so, she brought praise to God.

Now, my sister, I ask you: *Does your life magnify and bring praise to God?* As a Woman of Destiny, you must long to present your complete being as a living sacrifice unto the Father. You must be willing to live according to Romans 12:1, which says in the Amplified Bible:

I APPEAL to you therefore, brethren, and beg of you in view of [all] the mercies of God, to make a decisive dedication of your bodies [presenting all your members and faculties] as a living sacrifice, holy (devoted, consecrated) and well pleasing to God, which is your reasonable (rational, intelligent) service and spiritual worship.

Paul also said in Acts 17:28, "For in him we live, and move, and have our being..."

Oh, daughter of the Most High, I admonish you, magnify your God and lift up your life as a praise unto Him. For in the end, only what you do for Him will matter and be eternal throughout the heavens.

In closing, let me reiterate that God is calling you to be a true Woman of Destiny who:

Quality #5: Her Life Magnifies and Brings Praise to God

1) Fears not

2) Beholds the gifts within herself and walks in agreement with God's plan

3) Stirs up the gifts in other women

4) Is blessed because she believes, submits and obeys

5) Lets her life magnify and bring praise to God

My dear sister, God is calling you. *Rise up and be the Woman of Destiny God has called you to be!*

5 Qualities of a Woman of Destiny

Personal Reflections

Dear sister, take some time and reflect upon the questions below, responding quietly within yourself or within a journal.

1) What is the fifth quality of a Woman of Destiny?

2) How far back can the origins of your destiny be traced?

3) What sometimes happens when we wait for people to validate our destiny?

4) How important is aligning your soul to God's purpose for your life?

5) How can we magnify God with our lives?

6) Does your life magnify God? How?

*Quality #5: Her Life Magnifies and Brings
Praise to God*

Meditation For Activation

Meditate upon the following scriptures to gain and maintain greater success in your life.

Psalms 75:6-7 — For promotion cometh neither from the east, nor from the west, nor from the south. But God is the judge: he putteth down one, and setteth up another.

John 12:32 — And I, if I be lifted up from the earth, will draw all men unto me.

Romans 8:29-30 — For whom he did foreknow, he also did predestinate to be conformed to the image of his Son, that he might be the firstborn among many brethren. Moreover whom he did predestinate, them he also called: and whom he called, them he also justified: and whom he justified, them he also glorified.

Confession For Possession

I declare and decree I will magnify God with my life. I submit every part of my being to God's purpose for me. I decrease so that He may increase in me, releasing His Glory throughout my sphere of influence. My ways now become His ways, my thoughts His thoughts. I proclaim Him highly exalted in my words, deeds and actions. My will is to do the will of my Father, for He sent me for this purpose. I bring myself in complete alignment with God's destiny for me. Everything I am and am becoming will magnify and bring praise to Him. I am a God-appointed Woman of Destiny called to establish God's glory upon the earth! So be the Word of the Lord today! In Jesus' name, Amen.

About the Author

Tarsha is a dynamic, God-appointed Woman of Destiny who flows under a strong prophetic anointing. God has called Tarsha to teach His people who He is and their true identity in Him. With this mandate she humbly serves as a licensed minister, a compelling Bible teacher, inspirational speaker, certified Christian life coach, spiritual midwife, and ministry and business consultant.

Since childhood Tarsha has possessed a love for the truth and the meat of God's Word. It is through this love that God has birthed life-altering prophetic teachings that are reaching people from all walks of life around the world. Tarsha is most known for the powerful teaching series, *"The Woman in the Mirror"*, which has imparted life to those who desire to walk in their true identity in Christ. Her unique, illustrated teaching style has allowed many to "see" and "understand" what the Father is saying with complete clarity, practical application, and unprecedented spiritual breakthrough!

Tarsha is a published author. Her book titles include: *Called and Chosen: A Study Guide to Ministry*, *Help! I've Been Called By God: Easy Steps to Preparing and Delivering a Message*, and *5 Qualities of a Woman of Destiny*. God's vision for her life also includes helping other ministers publish their writings so she has launched Dominionhouse Publishing & Design, a publishing and graphic design firm dedicated to publishing the gospel with divine ingenuity and creative excellence. Tarsha is also the Executive Director of Revealed International Women's Empowerment Network, Inc., an organization dedicated to helping women unveil their God-given identity, potential, purpose, & destiny.

Tarsha believes there is nothing we can't do if we learn to tap into the divine mind of God and walk in who we really are in Him. She resides in the Orlando area with her husband of 22 years and their two children.

Contact the Author

Please email or write the author with any comments you may have. You are also welcome to contact her for bookings. As the Holy Spirit leads, Tarsha is available for book club presentations, signings, or speaking engagements for your church or organization (women's ministries, women's clubs, conferences, workshops, retreats, and seminars). Contact her at:

tarsha@revealedinternational.com
www.revealedinternational.com
www.womanofdestinyarise.com

P.O. Box 681938
Orlando, Florida 32868
407.880.5790

Do *YOU* know *YOUR LIFE PURPOSE...*
Why *YOU* were created and what is *YOUR DIVINE DESIGN?*
We can HELP YOU...

REVEALED INTERNATIONAL | WOMEN'S EMPOWERMENT NETWORK, INC.

Helping women unveil their God-given identity, potential, purpose, & destiny

Our passion is to empower women to embrace divine fulfillment through spiritual and personal growth and development.

YOUR LINK TO
SUCCESS & FULFILLMENT
Make the Connection!

WWW.REVEALEDINTERNATIONAL.COM

HAVE YOU BEEN CALLED?

Available now from DOMINIONHOUSE
Great for individual or group study

Help! I've Been Called By God: Easy Steps to Preparing and Delivering a Message has been designed to equip you. Whether you are a lay minister just starting out or a seasoned speaker, you will refer to this guide again and again! Within this book you will discover:

- An easy, step-by-step guide to preparing and delivering a message/sermon

- A tested and tried strategy for studying God's Word

- A simple, but effective approach to fasting and prayer

- An overview of the Five-Fold Ministry and much more

Order your copy today! Available at:
**revealedinternational.com
amazon.com, barnesandnoble.com, and other fine book retailers. Just ask for the book.**
ISBN-13: 978-0-9755234-0-7

The Mission of DOMINIONHOUSE Publishing & Design

**The Lord gave the word: great was the company of those that published it.
(Psalms 68:11)**

DOMINIONHOUSE Publishing & Design is dedicated to providing an outlet for those who have been "given a word." It is with this dedication to the Gospel that we offer quality custom publishing products and services, catered exclusively for the Body of Christ. It is our commitment to work cooperatively with you, the author, to bring the Gospel to the world, that we may experience DOMINION in all levels of living!

For more information about book publishing and our graphic design services, visit
www.mydominionhouse.com

Notes

Woman of Destiny

Notes

Woman of Destiny

www.ingramcontent.com/pod-product-compliance
Lightning Source LLC
Chambersburg PA
CBHW071318040426
42444CB00009B/2045